MW01252697

Anatomy Of My Poem

By Kenyatta McConico

ISBN-13: 978-1480132764
ISBN-10: 1480132764

For permission to use material from this text, contact the author at
kmcconico@hotmail.com

Visit and subscribe to

www.morning-prayer.com

Acknowledgments

"of a few of those who help to make me"

Thank you Misty, Alkebulan and Trinity Mae for being the inspirations of my life. Thank you also Deb, Chico, Byrd and Jimmy from whom I've learned so much and my friends who have been like brothers and sisters to me.

Thank you my Prairie View A&M University Family:
- ⅄ Omega Psi Phi Fraternity - Rho Theta Chapter
  - ° Fifteen True Soldiers / Tha '98
- ⅄ N'COBRA- Student Chapter
  - ° (National Coalition of Blacks for Reparations in America)
- ⅄ Michigan Club – Hometown organization

Special thanks to the late Dr. Imari Abubakari Obadele and Baba Hannibal Afrik who dedicated their lives to educating, fighting and preserving our people, my editor Yvonne Lopetrone for helping to complete such a task of correctly documenting a part of my life, and Rev. Thomas J. Cheeks and my St. Francis MBC family.

Table of Contents

Section I: Introduction
The Vitruvian Man 9

Section II: The Poems
The Observer 20
Religious..21
My Greatest Weakness..............................23
From Father To Son.................................25
Mr. Black and Mr. White..........................27
An Invitation To The Family Reunion.............29
My Call...31
A Slave Spoke To Me...............................33
Can I Share A Thought With You 35
Pimpology 101.......................................36
Akili's Grace..37
H.I.M. 39
Serve GOD, Not Man 42
Prophecy 44
Trepidation...45
Puppet Master 47
Can't Wait To Die 48
Because The Things We Long For
Are Not Always What We Need.....................49
I Don't Know If You Feel As I Do 51
Before I Die...53

Section III: The Anatomy

Psychoanalysis 56

The Observer (Commentary) 57
Religious (Heading & Commentary) 60
My Greatest Weakness (Heading) 63
From Father To Son (Heading) 64
Mr. Black and Mr. White (Heading & Commentary) 65
An Invitation To
The Family Reunion (Heading & Commentary) 68
My Call (Heading & Commentary) 71
A Slave Spoke To Me (Heading & Commentary) 75
Pimpology 101(Heading & Commentary....................81
H.I.M. (Heading) 85
Serve GOD, Not Man (Heading) 86
Prophecy & Trepidation (Heading)....................87
Puppet Master (Heading) 88
Can't Wait To Die (Heading) 89
Because The Things
We Long For Are Not
Always What We Need (Heading & Commentary) 90
I Don't Know If
You Feel As I Do (Heading) 92

Section IV: The Exercises
Today I 95
Sermon notes 96
Define your adversary 97
Speak and converse 98

Introduction
The Vitruvian Man

About the cover

I chose the base image, The Vitruvian Man, because at first glance all the observer sees is a naked man. This text is symbolic in that it presents me uncovered to the reader. By exposing my faults, weaknesses and innermost feelings about life situations I peel back the outer layers of myself. Superimposed on the chosen representation of my body is a halo, heart and the female body.

- The halo is a symbol of my spirituality, which is my strength. Through all of my studies and discoveries of religions I've remained a spiritual being. I find it most important to be consciously connected to THE CREATOR than connected to any one religion and its practices.
- The Heart is a symbol of my weakness. At times I believe we will make a decision or reaction based on our emotions rather than logic and reasoning. In most cases it is what brings about a negative outcome although it is the great power of love.

- The female body is the symbol of my primal instinct. More than female, the silhouette symbolizes the things I'm attracted to with urges whether positive or negative.

The Vitruvian Man was created by Leonardo Da Vinci based on the notes of Vitruvius Pollio who was a great architect, engineer and author. The drawing and notes together are also known as "The Proportions of Man" with the navel being at the center of the limiting circle defining man's physical reach into the universe. The cover image with my head upon the Vitruvian man and this text serving as the notes of my life gives the proportions of the man that I am with my physical reach into the universe being not much but my spirit, emotions and desires reaching much further.

<u>Slightly above failing</u>

This is my second book. In this text I decided to go back into my past to discover who I am. There was a question that I and a few of my college friends would say to each other at sporadic moments. The question was, "Have you found yourself yet?" I believe the question derived from the thought that we as college students had bought into the hype of college being the place where you were to find out who you really are and becomes the best years of your life. For the most part the question went without a definite answer for an answer like "I'm still searching or I'm not sure." In regard to college being the best years of my life, during that time I was convinced that they were definitely not. I graduated high school with a 2.5 grade point average and was now attending college simply because its colors were my favorite combination, purple and gold (I'll elaborate later). My experience in college was difficult because I had delved into a pool of determined, rich, intellectually prepared, highly sociable, ethnic group of individuals with promising futures and I had none of those qualities, so I thought. This crippling belief system had made me one of very few friends and an outcast of the socialites. With all of my hang-ups my first years of college became too familiar. I began to think, "This is just like high school or middle school, or maybe elementary." Then I thought, "Oh my GOD, this is my childhood!"

I had silently considered and labeled myself slightly above a failure a long time before college. I had revealed to myself that I did just enough to get by most of my life. My mother said I wrote chicken scratch, I half did things and I was lazy, and she was right. Ironically, I knew the results of being lazy but never made an honest attempt to get off my path of inevitable failure. Therefore, I was always only slightly above failing and knew that at the rate I was going I would eventually fail. Then, just as I predicted, I was soon on academic suspension. I had failed and it was entirely my fault. My mother had not requested that the school hold me back as she had done when I was repeating the 7th grade, because she felt I could do better. It was within my own power and I was so oblivious that I never came to the reality that I had failed. I discovered my failing by returning to school, still telling myself I need to do better, and having the head of the college refusing to sign my registration and telling me to go home.

Skipping class

I asked myself, "How did this happen? He just told me to go home!" I would now have to tell my mom that I was kicked out of college after she had bragged to everyone, including the church, that I was doing great in college. There in the Dean's office, I blanked out from the stress and my mind began to wander. I knew exactly how it happened, I thought to myself. It was because I did a poor job of my chores as a child. It was because I didn't apply myself like my 7th grade teacher said at the parent-teacher conference. It was also because barely passing was actually failing but with a teacher's compassion, earning nothing and I accepted it. I'll elaborate here on my story of

12

attending a purple and gold school. I began to come out of my shell in my senior year of high school. I had a job at a fast food restaurant, friends and a little popularity from pledging a high school social organization. I was also drinking to get drunk and skipping class. My getting kicked out of college was happening simply because I SKIPPED CLASS. It was revealed to me by an experienced skipper that a way to avoid security was to go into the library or career office and pretend to do some work. So one day my friend and I had to do just that. Security had seen our wandering as a bit suspicious so we needed to hide out until the bell rang. My friend and I decided to go into the career office. We lied and said we had permission to come and fill out college applications. We were directed to where the college information was and I learned that some colleges were pretty elaborate with their applications. So I took the ones that had some type of purple and gold in them. Genius, right?

So, going back to my meeting with the head of the college. He was going to just kick me out. He was justified with my previous bad grades in his hand and my silence. I had never been very vocal before but the thought of blowing an undeserved opportunity that many would love to have and the words "go home" changed me and that day I spoke two words, "I can't." I began pleading with him saying "I can't go back to Detroit without a degree. I wasn't focused before, I'll do whatever it takes to stay and redeem myself, and I also only had a one-way ticket and just got off the Greyhound bus. I'll be homeless!" He then gave me the option to either find a way home and serve my suspension at that time or retake the same course load and pass with decent grades but I would still have to serve my suspension the following semester. Of course I took the second option, got back in the line of several hundred students and registered for the same classes over again.

The semester went by quickly due to a lot less partying, drinking and things related to that other side of college life. When the semester ended I returned home and told my mother that I was suspended from school for a semester. I also told her that I would get a job, help with the bills and save to pay for my books, fees and transportation back to school and this time finish with a degree. I realized that although I had been in college, I was not a college student until I was prohibited from going to college. It was while I was vacuuming mud, crumbs, ashes and GOD knows what out of the floor of a rent-a-car that I realized that working at a rent-a-car place was not the life for me. I also realized that I was the only one with the power to change that. I began listening to motivational speakers, business start-up tips and reading the Bible while working overtime whenever I had a chance.

Co-Chair

When that next semester came around I didn't just go back to school, but I went back to school with a vengeance. I erased *I Can't* and *Failure* from my vocabulary. In fact when I hear those words today I feel physically sick. I began to complete assignments early instead of just on time. I found that by using my time wisely I still could have a social life but not like the one I had before. I began to see the campus differently because I was now participating. My participation was the exact opposite of my former self. Through participating I left my comfort zone and gained new friends. By socializing in more positive circles I learned that all the students were not rich, they didn't have it all together and they weren't all so intellectually prepared. They were more like me than I thought. The only difference was I allowed my preconceived notions to hide the real me from my surroundings and the generic me took over and was self-defeating. I learned that everyone had an ideal of who they wanted to be and were in college to find themselves in those possibilities. And they all had fears, but my fears were self-defeating. My returning to college was the death of my self-defeating nature. I was now activated. One of the organizations I participated in was N'COBRA (National Coalition Of Blacks for Reparations in America). N'COBRA is a powerful and determined organization on the national level. The education I got from this organization gave me a greater respect for Black History in America and a deep passionate concern for Black Futures in America. N'COBRA on the student level was to grasp the young minds and bring them in the reality of a crippling present that was brought on by an oppressive history and to unite and demand a brighter future. Our slogan was, "FREE THE LAND!" This is where I made my home. I was volunteering for events, attending seminars and passing out information. I was assigned to researching and giving updates on political prisoners. Soon there was an opportunity to become co-chairman of the organization, as the current co-chairman was approaching graduation. Before the meeting, where the voting was to take place, I had prepared a speech and picked out a shirt and tie and everything. When the day came around I realized that I had prepared to dress up for an environment that was pretty relaxed and was usually full of people wearing dashikis and head wraps. I finally decided to put on a decent button-up shirt and went and claimed my position as co-chairman. Co-chairman, because the office was designed to have both a male and female in position. I'm not sure how great a leader I was but I now had the chance to put into practice that there was no such thing as *I can't* or *failure.* My counterpart and I organized movie events, fashion shows, made newsletters and even transported a group to the Million Woman March, but my favorite was our poetry events. Our poetry events were where I was fully expressed. The place of dim lights, the smell of incense, low recordings of African drums and fruit smoothies was an outlet and an escape for me. It was the place where I could pour out my heart or express what was going on inside me and not be judged or fixed. People just listened, related, and clapped. I even proved that I had a little talent. This was a defining point in my life. I was doing something that I knew a few people enjoyed watching me do; more than that, I was sharing my true self; but even more than that, I was prophesying to myself.

I believe that because GOD created us in HIS image (Genesis 1:27) we are by default a substance of HIM. Being a substance of the CREATOR, when connected to HE our source, we too have the power to create. As gods (Psalms 82:6), (John10:34) we have the power to create. For GOD said "let there be" (Genesis 1:3) and by HIS will all was. So as we speak, by our belief, it shall be. I know now why I couldn't answer that old question "have you found yourself yet?" It was because all through college I was creating myself. So now if I were asked if college were the best years of my life, I'd reply, they weren't just the best years of my life, they were the prophetic years of my life! And as I look over these poems I see how they are now manifesting.

My mother often threatened, when she would find my or my brother's poems, to publish them herself and make a million dollars. I'm not sure if they are worth a million dollars, but here they are. My poems, published. Her prophecy in me.

The Poems

"that are my life"

<u>The Observer</u>

When night falls I'm active
and by day I'm reserved
As a nocturnal creature
only when the sun is down
can I act on the days urge

I can see better at night
whatever my vision takes in during the day
But let not my lack of sun
mean that of light, I'm afraid

Because it's not light, but enlightenment
I seek as I live and learn each day
And it's not that I hide in the shadows
I'm just more relaxed this way

At night I'm left alone
to reflect, meditate and pray
And prepare myself to learn
and observe another day.

By. Akili

<u>Religious</u>

What religion are you,
what rules do you live by
What steps are you to take,
to reach your place in the sky
Does your religion set your soul free
Are you an active member
of your tabernacle,
whatever it may be

Are you a religious person
if so, how can you justify
Is it because you've found a domination
that you think is right

I see your type every day
I watch you while you pray
You have the heart to tell others
that your faith is the only way

Christian, don't claim to live by GOD
when you only live in arrogance
Witness, don't claim you're working for a
new world
when that is all you work against
Muslim, don't try to influence my mind
when you're speaking
with a mouth full of swine
And then call yourselves religious

As though you never committed the crime

My motive is not to ridicule
or say that I'm right and you're wrong
I only hope that you are true
to the faith in which you belong

My denomination is none
but my religion is blessed
Because blessed are those who hunger
and thirst for righteousness....(Matthew 5:6,
NIV)

By Akili

My Greatest Weakness

She's strong, caring and loving
She's my greatest weakness
but I'm weak without her

She's indeed no simple woman
her mind is too strong
She's able to separate the sense from the
non-sense
because she has lived so long
I could never pull confusion over her eyes
because I love her too much to try
But even if I began an attempt
she would see through all my lies

She's my greatest weakness
but I'm weak without her

The mere thought of her
is to pass my heart and soul into her hands
and in the warmth of her embrace
I'm indeed a reduced man
She cares for me so much
in amounts I can't believe
So in order to keep her happy
I can only be what she expects me to be

You see she's my greatest weakness
but I'm weak without her

She is so full of love

Black Love, the kind not to be
underestimated
Love so pure and whole
and not to be dissipated
She encourages me, and helps me
in everything I do
No matter what troubles may come
her love will always be true

That's why she's my greatest weakness
and I'm weak without her
She loves me like no other but her.
GOD gave me a wonderful mother.

By: Akili

<u>From Father To Son</u>

Boy, what going on in your head
talkin' about you'd rather be dead
After all we've done for you
After Jesus died for you, I died for you too
Death is here to teach you
not mislead you

Thinkin' like you want to smoke weed and
act wild
'cause all of your friends, and not you, seen
juvenile
I already know you can't be a thug
'cause your heart bleeds your mama's blood

Instead, you got a chance to go to college
a chance to acquire world knowledge
a chance to advance and be a real man
and everyone, except you, gives a damn !

Don't tell me I don't know what you're
going through
Negro, I was young too
Using your friends as a reason to act a fool
when you need to be concentratin' on school

Son, don't let opportunity pass you by
and never be afraid to look the devil straight
in the eye
'cause he can only hurt you if you let him
but that don't mean you can just forget him

Take care of your business
so your mama can live comfortable at last
and quit punchin' that damn snooze button
and take your black ass to class !

By: Akili

Mr. Black and Mr. White

Hey there, Mr. White
How are you today, Mr. Black
*Oh ! I am just fine **these** days Mr. White*
Yeah! It's real peachy, cause these days..

There is no more answering to you
no more picking your cotton
no more shining your shoes
no more being a maid or butler at your
house
no more being whipped when we leave out
no more addressing you as sir or ma'am
because of the color of your skin
no more pitch forking hay to feed your damn
cows and horses
and getting stuck with them damn needles
and pins

Yeah, it's real peachy these days Mr. White.
So what exactly are you trying to say Mr.
Black ?

I'm saying, my people are on a rise
and getting better every day
we're going on to be businessmen, doctors
and lawyers
up from being slaves
we bout to crush you and take that white
pride away
see basically you ain't shit
yeah, that's what I'm trying to say

27

Mr. White: so what is **your** G.P.A ?

Mr. Black: fuck you !

Mr.: White (smiling) : Have a nice day.

By: Akili

An Invitation to
<u>the Family Reunion</u>

I have a question to ask
How are we to last?
How are we to last as a race?
when we can't unite
Once in history we came together
when it was time to fight

But what happen to that spirit
That spirit of Garvey, Martin and X
It seem that only a few of us
knew what to do next

It seem that only a few knew
that once we fought to move into the house
that we built in the first place
we also needed to take care of home
and improve our own space

Do you understand the question?

I restate, how are we to last?
We no longer know each other
We've become more like strangers than
friends or sisters and brothers,
or fathers and mothers
or even lovers

Answer me if you know me
but only if you know me

Only if you know you're a part of me
Only if you are my sister, brother,
mother or father
All in which, I have plenty
Because in all spectrums of my race
I have family

By; Akili

<u>My Call</u>

The time grows nearer,
but I'll move so slow
Each day fear tickles my heart a little more
but I'm more afraid not to go

I feel as if I belong there,

as though my mother's calling me back
to the land
But how can I return to some place,
 I never been as a physical man

My mind always leaves me behind
and my soul goes too
Doing things just as the elders
and as the native children do
I'm home
it feels like I never left
But I'm alone,
because actually I never went
So I vow that before I die
that's where some time will be spent

But I'm afraid
and I'll only admit it when it's true
What if for me the ultimate is due
For it is often said, if you take one step, he'll
take two

So now I'll pray, that HE will carry me the
rest of the way

And not drop me but place me on the other side safe
But what if my call home is a call home…

Well I heard it, and I'm on my way
I'm on my way to stand where my ancestors stood
and with their children I'll play
To finish the work my mind and soul started
and physically clean the mess they made
And to do the things I said I'd do
Before death comes my way

But "In the event of my demise"
rejoice!
Because we are not always sad when we pray
But rejoice knowing
I was on my way home anyway…

By Akili / Tupac

A Slave Spoke to Me

Tired from my day of doing nothing
I lay barely asleep
My mind restless and hungry for activity
but there was none for me
I put in the radio a cassette
the one with the slow and sad blues
And cracked the blinds
for a beam of moonlight
but still darkness filled the room
I don't remember when,
but at some point I fell asleep
Because I was awakened
by an icy cold breeze across my feet
I didn't get up, I stayed lazily in the bed
and suddenly the wind I felt on my feet
I felt softly over my head
At first, I thought someone came in the
room and turned the air conditioner on
But even though there was no one in the
room I did not feel alone
I felt the presence of people
more than just two or three
I felt a large crowd of people
of a hundred or more surrounding me
My eyes opened slightly
but it was still too dark to see
And that's when it happened

a slave spoke to me

As my sleepy eyes got use to the darkness

what I saw almost scared me to death
The adrenaline ran rapidly through my body
and my heart was beating too fast for me to
catch my breath
I froze and couldn't run
I thought I was good as dead
Because maybe there were more
still surrounding my bed
But that thought left me quickly
as I focus on the single silhouette
No shoes, no shirt, shackles on both wrist
and cloth pants extremely ripped
He never spoke to me in words
but I knew what he wanted to say
And when he felt I understood
he then faded away

Without words, he told me I was a King
and he was the reason for that
Because every brick I'll use to build my
Kingdom
he first carried on his back
He said one day I'll teach
those who were untaught
And one day I would lead
those who were lost
He said that I would be respected
as long as my respect last
And before I realized
it would have already come to pass.

By Akili

Can I Share a Thought with You?

Can I share a thought with you?...
I was just thinking that
the most beautiful thing in this world
could be you....
That being close to you
would be a great accomplishment
If I could do

At this moment nothing matters
I hear no noise, no machines, and no chatter
Just this pounding in my chest
which is the voice of my interest

I'm thinking that if you put yourself in my
arms
then you would feel as I do
May our thoughts become one and not two
May we integrate and create something true

Love

Love is my frame as I picture life with you.

Imagine that. A masterpiece
more valuable than anything
but yet it's free

Love can I share a thought with you?

By: Ken

35

Pimpology 101

Lovely ladies,
do you know the power you have
Do you know how important you are in a
man's life
The most beautiful creature on earth
even more sexy Black, than white

Without you we couldn't live
At least not in peace
because we have no love to give

And oh!, how gifted you are
An intellectual, brighter than any star
Gifted with emotions so complex
Gifted with true love much deeper than sex
And with a body so voluptuous
leaving any mere man in a sexual wreck

Do you recognize the power you have?
Do you recognize the power you have,
over man?
And now I have my chance …

Ha ! Ha ! Damn, you so dumb!
Because you lost it all
When I made you cum
And it was a part of Pimpology, Lesson 1

By: Akili

Akili's Grace

Akili: I can feel her in my presence, and
I'm honored to have her here
Such a woman of substance, of
tender loving care.
The combination that defines her is
what I love most of all.
Her capacity to love, her sweetness,
her beauty to never fall.
Never speak before a greeting
for my heart holds for her, a kiss
Subconsciously happy, what did I do
to deserve this

Grace: Excuse me; have you ever been truly
in love?
Akili: Have you ever been loved truly?
Grace: Have you ever been in her mind
instead of her body?
Akili: Have you ever been into him, and
put him for everybody?
Grace: Have you ever wanted to give your
all, but was afraid?
Akili: Have you ever wondered if you
really knew the person with whom
you laid?
Grace Have you ever cheated on the person
you truly loved?
Akili: Have you ever wanted to have sex in
a way that wasn't considered love?

Grace: Have you ever heard that song by

Prince "I Hate You or Damn You"?

Akili: Have you ever heard that song by
Rose Royce "I Wanna To Get
Next To You"?

Grace: Had you ever thought that maybe I
was attracted to you, in a way that I
knew we couldn't be together?

Akili: Had you ever thought that I felt the
same way so strong that I would
accept whatever?

Grace: Had you ever thought that you could
fall in love with me and my question
afterward, "would it still be
whatever?

Akili: Yes, I think I could fall in love with
you, and my answer to the latter
would be, *"never"*

Grace: I can feel him in my presence, and
I'm honored to have him here
Such a man of substance, of tender
loving care.
The combination that defines him is
what I love most of all.
His capacity to love, his sweetness,
his beauty to never fall.
Never speak before a greeting
for my heart holds for him, a kiss
Subconsciously happy, what did I do
to deserve this.

By: Akili & Grace

<u>He In Me</u>

Today was not a good day.

It may have been the worst day of my life
Everything managed to go wrong
even the things that are usually all right

Although I try not to exaggerate
for fear that I may say too much
But I could care less what happens
tomorrow even if I wake up

Already depressed, I laid down, my eyes
began to fill
realizing I just wished death on myself
and I'll surely die, if it be GOD's will

I remembered my mother saying "be careful
what you wish for you may get it someday"
I also remembered times before when I was
depressed this way my mother would hold
me and pray
And as we both cried
the pain faded away

But she wasn't here to do that for me now

So whatever, I'm not going to sit here and
cry like a baby
For that, I'm too old
And that night I went to sleep

without promising the Lord my soul

That night I had a dream
that seemed to be reality
I later found out it was of a future event
that would later happen to me

I dreamed I was sitting in church
on the pew where I always sit
And as the reverend was preparing to preach
the word
I had my bible preparing to receive it

She said,
" I want to talk to you about change this
evening, because some of us don't realize
that change is a perfect gift from GOD. And
all things will change except GOD.
Anything that grows will change and all
things will change because they grow. So
we should welcome change because it
signifies growth. And just as GOD promised
us the gift of change, he also promised us
that HE will never change. Turn your bibles
to James 1:17 where you will see …."

That sermon went on until she was done
and as soon as she finished I woke straight
up from my sleep
With just enough time to get dressed for
church
and maybe still get my seat

I figured I might as well go

and feel better about the previous day's
event
And rather than sit at home depressed
church should be time well spent

I made it in time to get my seat
and hear the preached word
But although the bulletin listed the Pastors
name
It was announced that Rev. Brenda Buckner
would be the next voice to be heard

She said;
" I want to talk to you about change this
evening, because some of us don't …."

I was stunned in disbelief
And I whispered the chapter and verse on a
whim.
And when she confirmed it
I thanked the lord I didn't wake up
But instead, it was **HIM.**

By:
Akili & Rev. Brenda Buckner

Serve GOD, not Man

The same air we breathe
since the breath of life
can be stirred into a twister
and sweep us away, day or night

The same water we drink
to hydrate our internal organs to live
can float "life" away in small bubbles
as our lungs give

The earth
in which our manufactured foundations bind
can be shaken loose
and swallow up mankind

Even the flame
we've learned to harness and generate heat
holds energy to consume even ourselves
at our defeat

These are the laws of GOD
that only he can give, and taketh away
and man can do neither
for he is weak and soon wither away

So when you preach unity amongst men
and feel yet alone
be thankful that GOD is with you

When you step forward
or others step back

don't worry because GOD stands with you

When something greater than you
inside you
speaks out *send me*
go willingly because GOD will go with you

And as The Great Shepherd leads
the lamb,
follow GOD
and your flock
shall follow with you

By: Dea.Kenyatta McConico

<u>Prophecy</u>

Who you want to be,
and who you'll become
may be two different things

I'm sorry to inform you
that you can't control what life brings

I can tell you that a force of nature
guides you
just as GOD wills it so

So where you need to be,
don't worry,
you'll go

There may be something positive
 in your future
as much as you try to go against the grain

So whatever future you believe suits you
Prophecy will remain the same.

By: The Spirit on the train

Trepidation

We learn from birth the power of the Most
High
yet we still stray from His word
We still have to be preached to, to be made
believers
searching for something we haven't heard

Sure we know what is written
'cause we read it ourselves
Yet facts from another source say a little
different,
so let's research to find something else

This path is dangerous
full of demons and angels too
You're asking for years and years of
confusion
and an unsettled soul to torment you

So should you stop now, I don't know
Should you keep going, I'm not sure
But many answers you'll find
may not all be pure

Unless you know GOD,
and add Him to your walk through life
Your soul will never settle
On the answers that are right

You already know what to do

simply practice what you preach
And then you can better administer
the things you teach

By: The Spirit on the train

<u>Puppet Master</u>

I know something you don't know
but maybe God told you too
You see the person you think you are
is not really you

The life inside your shell was never and will
never be yours
and I can tell you why
You were born for a reason
and for that reason you'll die

You see that reason is a secret
some will understand, and some will never
know
But you're helpless to a string of prophecy
just as a puppet in a show

By: Akili

Can't Wait to Die

Grief consumes my existence
but I knew this moment would arrive
Many wonders torment me
as I await in line

But question I cannot do,
because this is how it always been
They can't save themselves
so we must go to save men

Poor creatures, constantly suffering from
their own emotions
Not realizing the peace and happiness
that comes with devotion
Not realizing its power
against the beast of temptation
Cursed to live among demons
and devastation

But, I have a job to do
and there is no deviating from the goal
I must walk through this hell
until I save many souls

But it's so tiresome
I miss my pleasant and peaceful beginning
So I can only dream and imagine
until this awkward state has ended.

By : Akili

Because the Things We Long For Are Not <u>Always What We Need</u>

Because the things we long for
are not always what we need
I pray that the appropriate emotions always
supersede
those emotions that confuse infatuation
with relation
and pursue things not worthy of me

At this current time
when what I pursue is you
I long to make you my world
the reason I do what I do

I long to be everything to you
and you everything to me
Making you as important
as the air I breathe

I long to be your strength
so that your tasks are never too much
And to forever show you loyalty
and that I love you that much

Though I long to be what you want
and hopefully what you need
I ask the Lord to make me receptive enough

to allow you to be the same to me

But, because the things we long for
are not always what we need
I only know I need someone special in my
life, and I can see that in you, Misty

by: Akili

I Don't Know
If You Feel as
<u>I Do</u>

I don't know if you feel as I do.

But when I'm with you
the word sacrifice carries no weight
Whatever actions toward your happiness
 is now second nature
a reaction unable to hesitate

I don't know if you feel as I do.

But to me "forever" was something I could
not comprehend
But through time spent with you
I've gained new philosophies
and there are new things I believe in.

I don't know if you feel as I do.

But to me this word is no longer great
No matter how far apart we are,
just as GOD blessed the heart with love
she also blessed it to know fate

I don't know if you feel as I do.

Because to truly be inside you
is more than my mortal self can achieve
but you need only say "I do"

then I'll know
and we'll be.

By: Akili

<u>Before I Die</u>

I was born not knowing which way to go
not knowing which path to take
So I thank You for my Mother and Father
who guided me in Your Namesake

I knew not of the world
of what evils may cross my path
So I thank You for my Brothers and Sisters
who I've watched and learned on their behalf
Though I've sat and watched my friends and
even myself
walk a worn path through life
I know for everything received
there must be a sacrifice.

As I kneel and pray the best way I can
I hope that I have proved myself a man
I pray for no riches, no miracles
or pardons for the mistakes in my life
I only pray for one blessing
to receive before I die

That is the gift of eternal life
within the hearts of those I've touched
And even the ones I've tried
but continually missed so much.

Grant that I've completed my duties
that were set for me on earth
May I receive the honors
and the respect I deserve

When I've lived my life to the fullest
may my achievements not be in vain
But left behind to enrich my family
and those whose love for me still remains.
Amen

By: Akili

The Anatomy
"of my psyche"

<u>Psychoanalysis</u>

Through this poetical-psychological journey I hope to give an experience deeper than just reading poetry. Although I submit these poems for entertainment to be enjoyed they are a great part of who I am. In this section of the text I will attempt to search for the true meanings behind my poetry. I use the word *search* instead of *give* in the prior statement because there are always environmental factors that can be overlooked for all actions. The action in this case is the composition of poetry. Although poetry can be designed to have specific meaning it is still subjected to the influence of the poet's mental state, point of view and/or psyche. With this in mind I can only give you the meaning that is present on the surface but can search to find the deeper meaning below the surface.

Through my findings I hope to create a relationship with you. Our relationship is simply based on the human experience. So if you can relate to anything I've written in this book it is because you have, will, or are now experiencing it and through our experience I offer you enlightenment through my enlightenment and an awakening through my awakening.

The Observer

page 20

Original Heading
none

Commentary
In most of my poetry I would write a heading at the beginning that would serve as an introduction to the poem. The fact that there was no heading for this one means that it was written at the spur of the moment when I was probably observing something interesting in human behavior. Being an observer rather than a participator in this case speaks to my sociability. I've realized that at times I can be and seem to be very antisocial.

When I am antisocial it's usually because of my lack of comfort in the environment. This discomfort is brought on by the feeling that everyone is watching me, the belief that no one would be interested in what I have to say or that I'm just different in a strange way. There may be many other factors that come into play but the bottom line is that all of these things are created by us in our minds. They are just thoughts. When we are able to recognize when we are giving our thoughts too much power we can then control them. We can stop letting our imagination control so much of our reality.

So my exercise is to stop thinking and start doing. Approach someone with a few words, wait for a response and participate in the conversation. I can now quickly change antisocial to sociable at will. But to seem antisocial is a different monster.

When I seem antisocial I'm learning and processing my environment. But "seem" is a condition of being perceived by the environment, meaning it's outside of myself, and therefore I have no control over it. That which I cannot control, I give no worry to. Instead I'll continue to process the environment and after processing I can choose to participate or not. The choice to not participate is what causes the perception of being antisocial but only in that circle. The information that was processed can now be taken into a more comfortable circle of sociability or simply taken as a learning observation of people. This is the deeper meaning behind this poem. Take the line *I can see better at night, whatever my vision takes in during the day.* As meaning I can analyze and overstand in my seclusion what was presented to me throughout the day.

So as an observer I sometimes await an opportunity to socialize. Every day we have many opportunities to do something great for someone yet our inability or reluctance to socialize and truly understand the needs of people blocks us. This is what I observe every day. So here's an exercise (see pg. 94), seize a few opportunities out of the multitude to make someone's day by giving an interest to their need. One way to sense their need, without causing a discomfort in asking them, is by observing them. Helping someone I've observed is my way of projecting goodness in the universe And that which you project in the universe will come back to you.

__Religious__

__Original Heading__

Throughout my journey of life I've only found strength in one GOD. I shall worship no other. I can in no way ridicule any other religion. If I did so then I wouldn't be a man of GOD. I can only hope that the denominations keep their members faithfully in worship to GOD and not in confusion.

__Commentary__

I think this poem is pretty straight to the point. Hypocrisy! Although I remember writing this poem in college, I can't recall if it was fueled by any specific event. In a place where there are many people from many backgrounds there were many religions. Because so many religions were present none were easily detected unless the religion required a form of outward expression. For example, a female who wore the hijab was the clear indication that she was most likely Muslim. At most, the only indication of a person's faith was in the company they kept or their clear declaration.

We are judgmental despite how much we try not to be. We naturally gauge each other by appearance, demeanor, speech...etc., and treat each other accordingly. Unfortunately, who we are as a person is always hidden by who we are by appearance when there is no conversation. For example, someone told me that they thought of me as arrogant. They even went to a moment in history and described the event in which they came to that judgment. Within myself and others who knew me well, I was a very humble and modest person. I definitely didn't think I had anything in my personality or of my Person to be arrogant about. In the eyes of that person I carried that judgment until that later conversation.

But what happens when a person consciously pretends to be something that he or she is not? How dangerous is it to put on a facade and promote a false appearance? Could it be a dissociative identity disorder? Furthermore, what if the act was perpetuated by an outside force? In the religious arena I believe the danger lies in the influence of the person. Though we are all influential, and should be responsible for our public displays, a person who is constantly before the people can breed even more danger. For the average person is not particularly studied in their religion. Those individuals depend on the head of worship to give them accurate and true information. They also would expect the deliverer of the information to be a practitioner of it. This poem illustrates the practices of the religiously immature who attempt to affect others with doctrine that they do not follow themselves.

The amazing thing about this poem is there was a typo in the original that I accepted later as how GOD meant for me to write it. In the second stanza, I mistakenly typed the word "*domination*" instead of "*denomination*" like in the last stanza. Reading it now I see that it is correct in its error. For some will accept religion as a dominating factor in their lives instead of a faith freely chosen as a path to GOD. The person being dominated is now only good for two things: strategically winning over individuals to build the finances and numbers of a religious organization or to breed hate and separation in the world for different religious groups.

Here is an exercise (see pg. 95). Be inspired by the one delivering the message. But be inspired enough to take notes and study for yourself. Then after you study, whether there is confusion or not, go back to the messenger and discuss. Then the truth can then be found instead of dictated.

My Greatest Weakness

page 23

Original Heading

My mother was always there for me when I needed her and even when I didn't need her. She made sure that I knew that when the world was harsh and cruel I had a safe haven in her arms. Even when I felt I let her down or embarrassed her with my wrongdoings and didn't deserve her kindness, she loved me anyway and let me know that she always will.

Commentary

None

From Father to Son

page 25

Original Heading

My father died when I was young, and a part of me died along with him. I thought that I would never get that part of my life back. But now that I've gotten older I realize that I must live on, and in me my father lives on. One morning I woke with a new outlook on life as a result of a stern lecture from my father in a dream.

Commentary

None

Mr. Black & Mr. White
page 27

Original Heading

Our people, united, are the strongest on the planet. But some of us don't realize how strong we are or can be. There are some of us who fight for our reparations and then there are those who just want theirs handed to them.

Commentary

I can recall a day in college when I was visiting a friend to listen to some lectures from a pretty radical prophet. The prophet's words were very inspiring yet convicting. He spoke on a level that the average person would never quarrel with in the areas of ancient civilizations and religion. Although some things were hard to swallow, I understood why he appealed to the Afro centric audience.

One day, I met up with my friend in front of the cafeteria. It seemed there were visitors on the campus that day because I notice a lot of suits. I said "I wonder what's going on?", He responded, "I don't know, but I bet them white devils won't fuck with me no more! They tried to run down some shit on me as if I didn't know what was up. We are the original gods of this land!"

This was about the time where I was discovering conspiracy theories in many arenas. And in my discovering I came across some infuriating and sad events. Some of these events, on the surface, seemed to be whites against blacks, but beyond the surface was a case of the informed and misinformed. I believe sometimes individuals will allow outside forces to create enemies for them who indeed are not enemies at all. The misinformed will deem something or someone an enemy simply based on how it may have attacked someone else. The actions of the individual are now the reaction of the mind of that which misinformed them instead of their own mind. The misinformed mind has created a false enemy.

In this poem Mr. Black got some historical information that identified an enemy. Mr. Black then took this information and connected it to all the Mr. Whites of the world. Mr. White is now a false enemy created in the mind of Mr. Black. Mr. Black is now unable to put forth his real talent to Mr. White because of his false suffering at the hands of Mr. White.

Here is an exercise (see pg. 96). Think of something that you believe to be an adversary to your success. Write it down. Now think of how it has attacked you directly. Write it down. Now think of how is has attacked you indirectly. Write it down. Now think of how you may have suffered. How have you suffered due to the direct attack? Write it down. How have you suffered due to the indirect attack? Write it down. Now that you've written these things down and have them in front of you, you now have the information you need to deal with your adversary, and it came from you instead of outside of you. This means that ultimately you have control over all aspects of your success. You may also find that you as an individual cannot truly suffer from an indirect attack but you can choose to suffer from it, thus creating a false adversary to deliver it. Lastly, based on the information you've compiled is your adversary real or false?

An Invitation to the
Family Reunion
page 29

Original Heading

All that I've learned in my life was first taught to me by family. I feel that if when we have nothing, we at least have family. I also believe that we are headed to ruin because we have lost the respect for the family unit, our connection to each other as well as to Africans, Jamaicans, and other people of color….

Commentary

My family has reunions every year. So for a weekend in a different state the immediate families travel to visit to get to know their extended families. The event is filled with many things to do for all ages. So for this short time the distant relatives get together in love regardless of status, views, how well they know each other or even if they know each other at all. But after that it's "hope to see you next year" and back to our intimate circle of choice family members we enjoy. In contrasting a family reunion event with a race of people it's very similar. Of course we can unite over an injustice or a tragedy but what happened to a general and continuous care for each other?

I was born and raised in Detroit and I believed that I was ready to accept Detroit as the way things were. Then I began to travel and pay attention. I learned that Dearborn, Michigan was the largest community of Arabs and Arab Americans in the United States. I also learned that Greektown in downtown Detroit was just that, a concentration of businesses owned by Greek immigrants.

Furthermore, I learned that Frankenmuth, Michigan was like visiting Germany and all its customs. And these places are beautiful. And then I learned that American Africans thought of African Americans as lazy and Jamaican Americans had spots in pockets around the city that Blacks didn't patronize. And even more mind-boggling, an idea such as African Town could be shot down and deemed racist in a city that is in the majority, Black.

Through all the upsets in my observations I came to the conclusion that we have a problem when it comes to uniting in the spirit of building our communities. We don't show a general concern for each other's property or possessions. We suffer from egoism which only brings separation. So the question in the poem is *"How are we to last?"* for it is written "..every city or house divided against itself shall not stand"(Matthew 12:25. *KJV*)

Here's an exercise (see pg. 97). Speak. As I've seen in Houston, Atlanta, Washington, New York, Windsor, Toronto, Halifax, Egypt and Ghana, people of color speak to one another. They actually look each other in the eyes and speak, while looking someone in the eyes in Detroit can be taken as a sign of intimidation. So as often as you can, engage your distant brothers and sisters. Greet them in love just as you would greet an unknown distant relative at your family reunion. Only then will we see each other as family.

My Call

page 31

Original Heading

I love to travel. Sometimes I feel like I'm supposed to visit other places. I think of what awaits me, or what I'm to do once I get there. It haunts me, so I'll go and simply wait for the signs.

Commentary

Visiting Africa was a life changing experience. But it wasn't being in Africa that sparked the change in me, for my life began to change in the preparation for travel. This poem is an outline of what I was feeling leading up to the time for me to leave American soil. I was scared. Leaving the country was a major event in my life. And I wasn't just crossing over a river by bridge. Instead I was taking an airplane carrying over 200 people, more than ten hours over the Atlantic Ocean. The thought of it was mind numbing. But how could I miss this chance? This chance to visit the land of my ancestors, a place of such history. The motherland which I held so dear to my heart that it showed in my physical appearance. I can honestly say that near the time for me to leave my home I had totally put my life in GOD's hands.

To explain the first line, *The time grows nearer, but I'll move so slow.* I had a close friend help me with travel arrangements. My family helped me pack and made sure I had the medical and survival items I may need. And with all the help I had, I totally detached from the urgency and magnitude of the event. I had become so amazed that the day had come that my consciousness had split. It was similar to astral projection yet I was awake. I (spirit me) was conscious of myself (physical me) not being proactive but I could not motivate myself. I had completed a year of preparation by making payments, attending group meetings, getting shots and pills and researching travel arrangements to New York, yet when the day came I did nothing. And although I was excited in my spirit, my physical body didn't show it. In fact, I almost became a hindrance to myself. But it was meant for me to go and all obstacles were supernaturally removed.

First I wasn't sure how I going to get from the Greyhound bus station to the airport. The day before the time to leave a friend of mine, who knew about New York, helped to finish my travel plans. I had not factored in traffic and would have definitely missed the plane. Secondly, I left later than I was supposed to. I had a travel buddy who I was suppose to meet at the Greyhound bus station. But with all the last minute things I needed but forgot to get I was now running late. My friend who was coming to see me off picked up the things for me on her way to my house. Third, en-route to the bus station there was an accident on the freeway. I was sure everything was ruined then. I was on my cell phone with the person I needed to meet at the bus station telling her that I was on my way as they were explaining that the bus was loading and preparing to leave. My friend then decided to jump out of the car and approach an officer who was redirecting traffic. I don't know what was said, but I then had police escort through the traffic. Lastly, upon arrival to the station, I received a warm welcome from the unknown passengers who I was sure were furious and were enticing the bus driver to leave. My travel buddy had been holding the bus for me so some of the passengers knew we were traveling to Africa and were more relieved to see me than I had imagined.

I praised GOD for sending His angels to my aid. My spirit had connected to the center of the universe that governs all and not even I could stand in the way. Because the spirit operates on a higher plane the physical I had nothing to worry about. For this was predestined and was set in motion by my spiritual self. I only needed to let the supernatural complete it for me. I know now that this poem was, in essence, about astral projection. Take the lines,

My mind always leaves me behind
and my soul goes to

and

I'm on my way to stand
where my ancestors stood
and with their children I'll play
To finish the work my mind and soul started
and physically clean the mess they made

My spirit had already set this event in motion. I'm now a habitual meditator. Now, whenever I want something I pray and send my spirit to get it through meditation. In time, it is delivered unto me. I have an understanding now, that anything any of us wants we can obtain. If we focused our energy in the direction of our goal, the sea of obstacles would be parted and we'd walk to our destiny. Our faith would allow us to walk on water and tell mountains to move. For the spirit is not bound by anything on earth. Here is an exercise, I challenge you to sincerely pray, meditate and focus your energy on your desires. Keep in mind that this has little to do with any organized religion but everything to do with your spirituality.

A Slave Spoke to Me

page 33

Original Heading

I believe that all dreams carry a
message, especially the most peculiar
dreams. I also believe in the supernatural.
When our minds are relaxed and our
consciousness becomes subconsciousness
we open ourselves to a world of our own.
But can this world be entered? Can anybody
speak to the dead? Can the dead speak to us?
Our dreams make our thoughts and feelings
visible, maybe to answer what we don't
understand about ourselves or maybe to
awake us from an internal sleep.

Commentary

This poem was the beginning of life
for me. For a person to truly change or
gather a different perspective on life
sometimes a dramatic event must occur.
This was mine. This was my mind going
from extreme fear to perfect peace in a short
period of time. There are three elements that
made this experience such a defining
moment for me. First, the meditation,
second, the connection and lastly, the
message.

The poem begins with my day
winding down yet I was still feeling

incomplete and unaccomplished. But despite the case the day was still ending for me.   So I decided to give in and relax since my roommate was away and I had the room to myself. I began to create an atmosphere similar to a meditation room complete with dim lights and music. There may have also been incense. The only difference in my meditation room and others was the music I chose. The blues always worked for me because it invoked a feeling that although life, love and finance can be hard, everything would be alright, and that was my mental state as I went deeper into meditation.

The mind is an amazing thing, as it has the ability to store and recall information. It also has the ability to manifest your thoughts right in front of you. In regards to storing information the mind has infinite space. There is no amount of nanobytes and yoddabytes that can be compared to the mind. The challenge is accessing the information. Sometimes accessing information from the mind is triggered by some sort of external stimuli. For example, a person may recall a childhood event simply by a smell or image that is recognized deep in the corners of their mind. The event will then attempt to play-back in the imagination as if we had hit the rewind button on a video.

So what was created for me was triggered, recalled and then recognized as a person held in slavery by the things I had stored in my mind. But although this thing was created in my mind, utilizing my imagination, consider that imagination is a real thing yet to manifest. The thing that was created for me was a result of my current environment. I was around people who were proud and displayed their love for Black History, at a historically Black College which was built on a plantation with a preserved slave cemetery at the edge of the campus. I won't go as far to say that something came out of the cemetery to visit me but that those were the things that shaped my imagination. But what I will say is that meditation is the vehicle in which we can travel through the spirit world that is always present around us. Although the spirit world is not bound by anything in the physical world, it is in the in-between when something of the spirit may materialize in the physical. I had made a connection with a spirit in the in-between and it spoke prophecy in my life. The spirit was wrapped in an image that I respected and was familiar with through African American Studies but it gave a general message for my life. I feel that if GOD would have sent it in any other form it wouldn't have had a different effect on my life.

The message:

Without words, he told me I was a King
and he was the reason for that
Because every brick I'll use to build my
Kingdom
he first carried on his back
He said one day I'll teach
those who were untaught
And one day I would lead
those who were lost
He said that I would be respected
as long as my respect last
And before I realized
it would have already come to pass.

"He told me that I was King..." A prideful statement but humbling because I had not made myself King. This part of the message I needed to build my view of myself. In my first years of college I suffered from low self-esteem. Although exciting, I was traveling to a place I knew nothing about. There were no friends or family available for me on campus and I was holding on to a long distance relationship. I wasn't very sociable so I spent a lot of time withdrawn from my new environment. I'm thankful to the people who were friendly to me because I began to open up to them and they accepted me for who I was. As time went on and I became more involved and who I was made me more visible to others. I found that I could be inspiring, strong, influential and empowering. My environment began to shape me. Soon it presented pedestals and some I accepted.

"He said one day I would teach..."
My assignment. Although I now have a
career in education it was the furthest thing
from my mind in my college years
especially since I was lacking in that area.
But I know now that this verse was much
deeper than just becoming a teacher. It was a
prophetic example of divine intervention.
The career I chose was not the one that
chose me. And the one that chose me was
set before me by the historical record of my
gifts and talents. I found, when called to
perform, I was able to deliver information in
a way that was easily understood. Some
people even asked my advice or view of
things to help them make decisions. So,
although strange at first, being in front of a
group of students brings out the best in me.
Now I look forward to teaching, counseling,
speaking, presenting, and authoring for it
gives me a chance to share myself with
others.

"He said I would be respected..."
Assurance. As the saying goes "Respect is
earned, not given." I never really share too
much of myself because I didn't think I
would be respected. To me the greatest
feeling of defeat is knowing that you've
poured your heart into something for it not
to be received well. I didn't want to ever feel
that so I kept my talents to myself. The fear
and embarrassment that came from not

being heard or, even worse, purposely ignored, is the stuff that makes haters. Individuals who are overbearing in their speech and quick to look down on someone who they perceived as threatening competition suffer from this fear. My being soft spoken wouldn't survive in such environments so I shied away. Such a lonely existence. But as I matured and got involved in more things I found that my silence was my strong point. My silence is what intrigued people the most, my tone was low and my language respectful. I found that I was respected more than I believed for I was earning it all the time by not being that person who was labeled "Talking loud and saying nothing." But the challenge was to remain respectful. I was careful to remain humble and not abuse all that I receive by showing arrogance for such has brought down kingdoms. I learned that I had to make people feel as important as they made me feel, as special as I felt to them, as loved as they loved me. This tradeoff between everyone and me is what continues to build my character and ultimately my success.

Here is an exercise. In your daily encounters with people try hard to gauge their positive perceptions of you and give that back to them doubled. For example if they are giving to you then give to them twice as much.

Pimpology 101

page 36

Original Heading

I am one who believes that women and children are the future. To me, the turnout of our people becoming successful figures of the universe depends on the strength of women but do women think so? Some women lose sight so easily and for what? *Recognize the power you have.*

Commentary

Needless to say this poem came from a place of immaturity and pain. The strange thing about my reading this poem again years after I wrote it is that I can see the immaturity but I didn't know I was hurting. I can even recall reading *"Pimpology 101"* at an event in college and how it was received. The audience applauded. Someone even said, *"I loved how you just switched it on 'em and put'em in check"* Although I may have delivered it dramatically and hid behind the heading of the poem, that I also read to the audience, the deeper meaning is the hurt I felt my first semester of college and how I acted out in my second.

In my first year of college my grades were pretty good. I was focused on doing a good job in school and not being distracted by campus life. My view of campus life as a freshman was drinking, parties and girls, but I was a dull boy in that respect. One reason is that I was holding on to a long distant relationship. I felt my relationship was going great. We talked often and sent cards. The constant contact between my girlfriend and me comforted me and I remained faithful in the midst of all the voices around me. I also made an effort to keep the drinking and partying at a minimum as I felt I would only subject myself to temptation. I would say to anyone that a long distance relationship takes a lot of work and a great deal of that work is being truthful and authentic with your partner but most of all yourself. So toward the end of the semester the anticipation began. I couldn't wait to get home to my woman. But once home the reunion wasn't so dramatic. Of course we were glad and excited to see each other but with each day the feeling faded more and more. Finally one day she said it, "I had to break up with Frank." What ?, Who is Frank !?, I replied. It's important to say that I don't mean to put my ex in such a terrible light for I can't say how she felt being away from me for months, or when she was expecting me to call some nights and I didn't. But in any case my girlfriend became someone else girlfriend.

During my second year I became a totally different person. I celebrated my freedom recklessly. I walked the campus with pimp theme music in my head like *Mark Morrison – "Return of the Mack."* From an inauthentic relationship I became inauthentic. I gave women the person I thought they wanted and trusted no one. This was the characteristic that wrote *"Pimpology 101"* Accepting no responsibility for my actions or broken hearts. Needless to say this was the semester of partying, drinking and meaningless relationships,"The 10." I still had love but only revealed it to a chosen few.

In this phase of my life I also encountered a different type of woman. The type that was just as reckless and the type who just accepted it as though she didn't deserve better. I began to think that I had been naive and wasn't living because I thought that all women wanted to be loved and exclusive to one person. I probably would never understand and won't pretend now, the good girls that love bad guys or the bad girls who gave in to hopelessness. Those are the ones who give up or don't recognize the power they have. I've learned now that I wasn't being naive, I was just being myself. I still believe that deep down everyone wants monogamy and can be monogamous it just may be easier or protective to the heart to be someone different to someone else.

I soon came to my senses and spent the majority of my college life with one woman, not because I was naive but because that was who I was and who I am. I also can't leave you, the reader, with a thought that long distance relationships don't work, they just take work. I know that a long distance relationship can work, for me and the one I married, who is mother of my children, and who is loved by my family and friends, nurtured our relationship while we were living in different countries. My challenge to you is to ask yourself in all relationships whether they are romantic, friendly, business related or community related, are you being who you are? Are you being authentic, because that is the key to any of your relationships lasting.

H.I.M.
page 39

Original Heading

Depression is universal. Each one of us will go through it in some form or another. Yet, when we go through it, it feels as if it's only happening to us. I was inspired to write this poem during church while the associate pastor was discussing coping with change. At the time I was depressed about something and her sermon helped me to deal with it. After church I told her that she inspired me to write a poem and I would give it to her the following Sunday. But I didn't attend church that Sunday nor did I get past the one line I started. During those two weeks my depression had faded but I began to focus on my niece. She had suffered a loss that began a domino effect in her life. In such a short time she had lost so much. It was a depression I couldn't understand. After sitting with her Saturday evening, later that night I finished the poem and gave it to the pastor Sunday morning. For Tanisha.

Commentary

None

Serve GOD, not Man

page 42

Original Heading

The average church goers may never understand what goes on behind the sermon. At least for me, I was never mindful of the stress that can be brought upon the pastor of the congregation. Generally, I figured that it was the deacons and trustees' job to handle all matters of the church while the pastor concentrates on delivering the word. I guess that's why I'm the deacon I am. The type of deacon who is willing to step in whenever possible to protect the heart of the pastor. Not to say that other pastors don't, but I've witnessed my pastor give much of himself to counseling, visiting, loaning and sacrificing even his minimal compensation for members of the church. At times he seems to serve man with the time and life he dedicated to GOD. I wrote this poem to encourage him remain focused on GOD in spite of all the worries that the congregation may bring. For man is fragile and flawed, and can only be strengthened by GOD to be a leader who leads effortlessly by the support of those who follow.

Commentary

None

Prophecy & Trepidation

page 44 & 45

Original Heading

Strange things can happen when you're alone with just your thoughts for a good period of time. Travel is as important to me as education. I believe it is education, and also time to relax, analyze and regroup. After finishing a great religious book I decided to retreat to the diner car to write a poem. And there I was spoken to yet the voice of thought, the voice of angels, or the voice of God seemed to be the less confused voice of myself. Two poems came out of me that night that were off the subject I planned to write about.

Commentary

None

Puppet Master

page 47

Original Heading

I've always believed that everyone and everything has a purpose. Even if that purpose is just to be seen so others can make a decision. God doesn't create pointless beings…

Commentary

None

Can't Wait to Die

page 48

Original Heading

Throughout my life I've been told that I could or will be a preacher, but I couldn't believe this for myself. Others have always found comfort in me, or wanted to know my views of things. Then one day in Africa someone told me that I was maybe given a mission and that "no matter how hard I try not to, I'll do it, can't help but to do it." Have you ever felt a separation from mankind you couldn't explain? ……
Dedicated to Hannibal Afrik

Commentary

None

Because the Things We Long For Are Not Always What We Need

page 49

Original Heading

One night I was inside a club and met someone who was the exact image of a woman I've dreamed of before. So I found courage enough to talk to her and she smiled back. But there was only one thing that stood between us, the elements earth and water. This is for my Canadian.

Commentary

GOD blessed me to be a premarital counselor for a few couples. This ministry allowed me to explore the desire of love between two people as well as analyze and evaluate my own marriage. Serving in this capacity was evidence that the things we do for others in spirit of GOD are not necessarily for them but also for ourselves. This poem attempts to illustrate the battle within the heart that seeks true love. I believe that every one of us seeks the comfort and security of a loving monogamous relationship. Yet this desire is threatened by not actually knowing if the other feels the same. Of course we say and even do things that seem to support our feelings in the beginning but dating can be so temporary.

It's always great to meet someone new. The enjoyment we get from simply being friendly with someone just encountered. Whether it be a social gathering, share a conjoined seat in travel or an introduction from a mutual friend, the stranger is so intriguing. And they "the stranger" can be frozen in time in our minds as "fun" in whatever event that took place. I believe that we will sometimes forget that the image that we've frozen in our minds represents a real person in the physical world. And all things in the physical world change or grow with time. The best we can do is grow with them. Even the Bible states in Genesis 2:24 "Therefore shall a man leave his father and his mother, and shall cleave unto his wife: and they shall be one flesh (KJV)." Since flesh cannot grow apart from itself neither can the husband and wife.

I feel blessed that GOD has used me for those couples as they are still happily married. I stay in continual prayer that HE keeps my wife and I growing forever more together till death do us part. And that we never create complacent images of each other in our heads that we put forth no effort in making the other happy.

This poem is definitely linked to "*I Don't Know If You Feel as I Do*" which is a poetic proposal long before the actual.

I Don't Know If You Feel as I Do

page 53

Original Heading

I've heard before that "when that one comes along you'll know." But how will you know? I've seen too many relationships fail to the point where I'm not strong enough to believe in my own. But maybe I've just been too preoccupied with that philosophy.
Maybe you can only really know by trusting what is in your heart.

Commentary

None

Exercises

"Do the worksheets"

Today I ...

Directions: Use this table to record your feelings after seizing a moment to do a good deed for someone.

Today I feel blessed	While driving to work I saw someone standing in the rain waiting on the bus. Although I couldn't give him a ride, I stopped and gave him my new umbrella that was still in my trunk unused

94

Directions: copy this page and use it to record notes from the
messenger while at your place of worship.

Study Notes

Topic_____ Date_____

Scripture(s): _____

Notes:

_____
_____
_____
_____
_____
_____
_____
_____
_____
_____
_____
_____
_____

Questions:

_____
_____
_____
_____
_____
_____
_____
_____

Defining your Adversary

Directions: Use this table to record and study what you feel may be hindering your success. *Although the poem makes an individual an adversary, note that Mr. White may represent a fear of corporate America. With that in mind understand that our true adversary lies deep within.*

Adversary		Description	Is Direct	Is Indirect
Procrastination	Attack	I've allowed my procrastination to hinder my completing projects. (to counter this attack I will keep some sort of schedule giving me a time frame to work on projects)		
	Suffered	I may have hurt my credibility with others because of procrastinating (To counter this attack I will communicate with other to ensure their satisfaction in my service)	X	X
Adversary	Attack	I have not had time to take on other project (Scheduling myself will make time for me to take on more projects)		
	Suffered	I may not have been suggested to others by others (I shall strive for quality in my services that others might promote me)	X	X
Adversary	Attack			
	Suffered			
Adversary	Attack			
	Suffered			
Adversary	Attack			
	Suffered			

Directions: Look someone in the eye and speak, maybe even engage them in a little small talk. Try to engage five people you don't know a day.

How many people did you speak to today?

~~IIII~~						

Notes:

_____
_____
_____
_____
_____

How many people did you engage in conversation?

Notes:

_____
_____
_____
_____
_____

More titles by
Kenyatta McConico

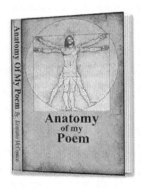

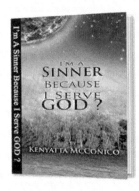

Get
them
all !

www.morning-prayer.com

Toast Masters Ice Breaker Speech

I understand an ice breaker to be an opportunity to open up and tell someone about yourself, inviting them to began a relationship with you.

So I'd like to introduce myself and I'd like for you to remember that I'm a product of Detroit.

My name is Kenyatta McConico and I'm a product of DPS (Detroit Public Schools). I also hold a Bachelors in Industrial Technology and a Masters in Business Administration. Because I find education so important I believe it was only natural that I ended up teaching for over 12 years, ended up moving on to become a Chair of the School of Design and Drafting at ITT Tech and an entrepreneur in the industry of Graphic Arts.

I also love to travel and it's funny how people respond to you when you're from Detroit. So when I traveled to Africa and visited both Ghana and Egypt, I was amazed to be engaged in conversations about the historical

Underground Railroad site in downtown Detroit, and its many stations about the city that lead all the way to Halifax, Nova Scotia, which is the hometown of my lovely wife.

I'm also ambitious about spreading awareness, which is what brought me to Toastmasters. Because in an environment where there is a lot of people talking loud and saying nothing it's hard to hear someone who speaks softly although they may be saying much. I often think about the younger generation who are misled by the media who could benefit from a mentor who helps them discern reality from fantasy. Or autistic children, like my 3 year old son, who may lose a chance at early intervention because of the lack of advocacy in the inner-cities. So maybe through practicing here I can become one who speaks loud and says much to benefit others and enrich myself.

So once again I'd like to introduce myself. I'm Deacon Kenyatta McConico and I would like for you to remember, I'm a product of Detroit.

39966361R00057

Made in the USA
Lexington, KY
25 May 2019